Carol Deacon's Little Book of
Easy Christmas Cakes

Carol Deacon CAKES

CDC Publishing

www.caroldeaconcakes.com

Introduction

It was the Victorians who started the English tradition of a rich decorated fruit cake but its history goes much further back in time than that. In fact its origins can be traced right back to the beginnings of Christianity when a special porridge would have been made and eaten on Christmas Eve to celebrate the end of a day of fasting.

Traditions evolve and change with each generation and as our world gets faster, more furious and commercial, some of the simple charming pleasures such as baking can get trampled, overlooked and discarded.

Christmas has always been a special time for me as it's also my birthday (Christmas Carol – get it ?!) which is why continuing some of the Christmas Customs seems especially important to me.

With supermarket shelves groaning under stacks of ready made cakes, decorating your own cake is an easy part of the Christmas build up to avoid. But to do so means you miss out on a little bit of Christmas magic. The chance for you and your children to stir the cake mixture and make a wish, the chance to fill your house with the wonderful spicy Christmas aroma of cooking cake, the chance to either start or pass on your own family Christmas traditions.

Yes I know it's a time of stress and chaos too but your cake can be baked as early as October and decorated in late November when you might have a spare evening or two to have a go.

All these cakes have been designed with simplicity in mind. You can make them as easy or as complicated as you like. You need only have one snowman or penguin on your cake if you wish or you can have a whole town's worth. If you think that covering a cake board looks too complicated, avoid it and leave it plain or use a ribbon instead.

Above all remember that baking and cake decorating should be therapeutic and enjoyable and besides, if it all does go horribly wrong you could always resort to the aforementioned supermarkets and buy one!

So have a go and as you do, and look on the bright side. At least I'm not trying to encourage you to decorate porridge!

Happy Christmas Cake Decorating.

Carol Deacon

Contents

Baking Your Christmas Cake

The thought of baking your own Christmas fruitcake can seem quite daunting if you have never done it before because there seems to be so much mystery and hard work surrounding it.

In theory it should be baked in October then "fed" with a little rum or brandy once a week. This allows the deep flavours to mature and intensify. In practice, mine is usually made a couple of days before Christmas and decorated as soon as it's cooled!

The secret is to read the recipe through first, then gather and weigh everything beforehand. That way you're not scrambling about the kitchen, opening cupboard doors with sticky fingers and falling over dogs and small children who always seem to surface when anything interesting is going on in the kitchen. The recipe in this book is the one I always use but feel free to use your own favourite or traditional family recipe if you prefer.

I don't have room to print them all here but there is a collection of other fruitcake recipes on my website some of which take into account special dietary requirements. The website also deals with amounts for other cake sizes.

You can make a fruitcake either by hand or by using a food mixer. Just make sure the butter is nice and soft before you start especially if you're hand mixing.

The fruitcakes in this book are all covered first with marzipan (almond paste) and then with sugarpaste (also known as Ready-to Roll Icing or Rolled Fondant)

If no-one in your family likes fruitcake, you could substitute a vanilla or chocolate sponge cake instead. All the designs in this book would work just as well on a sponge cake.

If you decide to use sponge cake as a base, split, fill and cover it with a coating of buttercream. You will then only need to cover it with sugarpaste. (rolled fondant) You will not need to use marzipan. Full instructions and recipes are available on the website **www.caroldeaconcakes.com**

Christmas Fruitcake Recipe

This recipe will fill your home with a wonderful Christmas aroma as it cooks. If you are using a fan oven that allows you to cook with the fan off, then do so as the fan can dry the cake slightly. If your cake cracks whilst cooking, don't panic ! You will be covering it anyway and any unsightly areas can be cut away before the cake is decorated. The recipe given here is for a 20cm (8in) round cake.

175g (6oz / 1 heaped cup) currants
175g (6oz / 1 heaped cup) raisins
175g (6oz / 1 heaped cup) sultanas (golden raisins)
45g (1½ oz / 3 tbsp) mixed peel
75g (2½ oz / heaped ½ cup) glace cherries
150mll (5 fluid oz) either brandy, rum, sherry or fruit juice

Put all of the above in a bowl. Place a lid or plate over the top and allow to soak overnight or for at least four hours, stirring occasionally. After that time, the fruit will have soaked up the liquid and be glistening and plump – all ready for the next stage.

175g (6oz / ¾ cup) soft butter
175g (6oz / 1 heaped cup) soft brown sugar
4 eggs (medium)
200g (8oz / 2 cups) plain flour (all purpose flour)
2 tsp mixed spice (apple pie spice)
½ tsp cinnamon
½ lemon (zest only)* Optional
30g (1oz / ⅓ cup) ground almonds
30g (1oz / ⅓ cup) flaked almonds (slivered almonds).

Baking time 1 hour 45 minutes (approx).

* Lemon zest is simply the yellow skin. To avoid unnecessary pesticides, try to use organic, unwaxed lemons and use a tool called a zester to scrape it off.

Lining your Tin

You will need a 20cm (8in) round cake tin (pan) with or without a loose-bottom - it doesn't matter. A roll of baking parchment or greaseproof paper (waxed paper), a ball of proper string (not plastic or it will melt), pencil and scissors.

While the fruit is soaking, prepare the cake tin. Because it has to cook for such a long time, the tin for a fruitcake needs to be double-lined to stop the sides scorching before the inside is fully cooked. You can use either greaseproof paper or baking parchment (baking paper).

1 Using your tin as a template, draw round and cut out three discs the same size as the base of the tin.

2 Cut two long strips of parchment or greaseproof 66cm X 20cm (26in X 8in). Fold one in half lengthways and stand around the outside of the tin. Tie a piece of string around the outside of the tin to hold it in place.

3 Fold the second long strip in half and stand inside the tin. Finally place two discs on the base other inside the tin. Your tin is now ready for action !

TIP: If you find lining the inside of your tin too fiddly, you can also buy paper cake tin liners in a variety of shapes and sizes from cake and kitchen shops. You will still need to wrap a strip of greaseproof around the outside of the tin though.

Making and Baking

1 Pre-heat the oven to 150° C / 300° F / Gas mark 2. If using an electric fan oven, I would suggest dropping the temperature to 130° C.

2 Beat the butter and sugar together until creamy. Beat in the eggs one at a time.

3 Sift the flour and spices into a separate bowl and slowly stir it into the mixture. If it still looks a bit runny stir in a little extra flour.

4 Stir the lemon zest and almonds into the soaked fruits and slowly stir into the cake mixture.

5 Spoon the mixture into the prepared tin and gently smooth the surface. Cut a small hole out of the centre of the last remaining paper disc and place it on top. This stops the top from browning too quickly. The small hole allows steam to escape.

6 Place the cake in the centre of the pre-heated oven. Bake for about 1 hour 45 minutes then remove the paper off the top. Lightly prod the top of the cake if it feels very soft and you can still hear a lot of bubbling it is not cooked. If it looks done and feels firm to the touch, insert a skewer or sharp knife. If it comes out clean, the cake is cooked. If it's not, give it another 15 minutes cooking and test again.

7 Allow the cake to cool completely in the tin before turning out.

Storing

Your fruitcake can be stored for up to three months.

Once cooled, pierce a few holes in the top with a cocktail stick and drizzle a couple of tablespoons of brandy or rum over the top. Then double wrap the cake in two layers of greaseproof paper and two layers of aluminium foil.

It will then sit quite happily on a shelf in a food cupboard until required. You can "feed" your cake by spooning over a little more alcohol every 7-10 days if you wish.

Do not store in a plastic airtight box or your cake will sweat.

Basic Equipment

**Not everything here is essential and much of it you may have around your kitchen already.
Build your collection up gradually.**

1 Mixing Bowl
A large bowl is essential for mixing cake mixture and icing.

2 Wooden Spoon
Used for stirring cake mixture. The handle can also be used as a modelling tool.

3 Small Bowls
Use for holding water and icing sugar when decorating.

4 Teaspoon
For stirring and spooning small amounts of ingredients.

5 Cutters
Available in metal and plastic, there is a huge range available. Collect them as you go along. No cutters are essential for any cakes in this book.

6 Rolling Pins
A large rolling pin is essential for rolling out marzipan and sugarpaste. A small one is useful for small quantities but a paintbrush handle will work just as well.

7 Small Non-Serrated Knife
A small sharp knife with a straight blade is vital for neat clean cutting.

8 Paintbrushes
You need a medium brush for sticking models and a fine one for painting details. Sable brushes are expensive but are best and will last for ages. They are soft enough not to dent the sugarpaste and have a fine pointed tip for delicate painting.

9 Pencil
For tracing and drawing templates.

10 Drinking Straw
Use as tiny circle cutters for making eyes. Held at an angle and pressed into an icing face, you can also use them to make smiles or frowns.

11 Pastry Brush
Used for spreading apricot jam over the fruitcake and moistening marzipan with water. You can also use them dry as a brush to gently clean your cakes.

12 Cocktail Stick
Use these to add food paste colour to sugarpaste. They can also be rolled over sugarpaste to make frills.

13 Spatula
Use for getting cake mixture and icing out of bowls.

14 Carving Knife
Use for slicing and shaping cakes.

15 Palette Knife
Useful for spreading jam and buttercream and loosening rolled out sugarpaste stuck to your work surface. Also makes a safe knife for small children to use.

16 Cake Smoother
Helps achieve a professional smooth finish when covering cakes with sugarpaste.

17 Tea Strainer
Useful for sieving small quantities of icing sugar "snow" over small areas.

18 Sieve
Use to sift lumps out of flour and icing sugar. Push icing through it to make good hair!

19 String
Tied around the paper on the outside of a baking tin when cooking fruit cake.

20 Turntable
Not essential but it does make cake decorating easier.

21 Scissors
Used for cutting string, tape and around templates

22 Small Plastic Food Bags
For storing sugarpaste and marzipan to prevent them hardening.

23 Tape Measure
Use for measuring circumference of boards and cakes and measuring ribbon.

24 Sticky Tape
Use a little bit at the back of a cake to hold ribbon in place.

25 Baking Tin
Used for baking cakes.

Covering Your Christmas Cake

To make things simpler for you, all the designs in this book use a 20cm (8in) round cake. In one set of designs, the cake is a normal flat-topped cake. In the other set, bits have been carved out of the cake prior to decorating it to give it an irregular shape. You can use either style of cake for any design.

The fruitcakes are covered first with a layer of marzipan and then with a layer of sugarpaste (also known as ready-to roll icing or rolled fondant)

Covering a Flat Round Cake

You will need

1Kg (2lb) marzipan
1Kg (2lb) white sugarpaste (rolled fondant also known as ready-to-roll icing)
2-3 tablespoons brandy or rum
3 tablespoons boiled apricot jam
1 cup cooled boiled water
Icing sugar for rolling out

Equipment

Carving knife
Pastry brush
Small heatproof bowl
Rolling pin
Cocktail stick
Cake smoother (optional but useful)
Small sharp, non-serrated knife
25cm or 30cm (10in or 12in) round cake board

1 Remove all the greaseproof wrapping. To make the cake level, carefully slice and remove the domed top off your cake and turn it upside down on your cake board. Fill any obvious holes with little balls of marzipan.

2 Pierce the top a few times with a cocktail stick. Drizzle the brandy over the top and allow it to sink in.

3 Place the apricot jam in a heatproof bowl and either microwave on high for 2 minutes or stand in a pan of simmering water until it boils. Then "paint" the jam over the top and sides of the cake. This will glue the marzipan to the cake.

4 Dust your work surface with icing sugar and knead the marzipan until pliable. If it is really cold and hard to work with, you can microwave it for 10-15 seconds. Test it and repeat if necessary for a further few seconds. Do not over heat it though, as the oils in the marzipan can get very hot and could cause a nasty burn.

5 Sprinkle more icing sugar on your work surface and roll the marzipan out to a thickness of about 5mm (¼ in). Lift and place it over the cake.

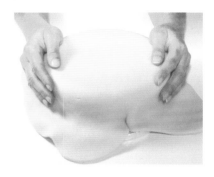

6 Starting with the top of the cake (so that you reduce the risk of trapping air bubbles) smooth the surface of the marzipan. A cake smoother is a useful tool for doing this. You use it like an iron to literally "iron" any wrinkles out.

However, keeping your hands flat, you should be able to use the heels of your palms to make an acceptably smooth surface.

7 Smooth the sides of the cake and trim away any excess around the base with a small sharp knife.

8 Lightly brush the marzipan with the cooled boiled water. This is to make it tacky so that the sugarpaste will stick to it.

9 Dust your work surface with icing sugar and knead the sugarpaste until pliable. Roll it out and lift and place over the top of the marzipan.

10 Again starting with the top, smooth the icing in place then do the same with the sides. Trim and neaten around the base.

Covering an Irregular - Shaped Cake

Because there's no need to make the top and sides perfectly smooth you can cover both the cake and board with sugarpaste in one go. The "You Will Need" and "Equipment" lists are the same as for "Covering a Flat Round cake" above.

Use an additional 200g (7oz) sugarpaste if you are using a 25cm (12in) round board as on the "Snowmen" cake.

1 Remove the greaseproof wrapping from the fruitcake and carefully carve a few dips and hollows into the top and sides of the cake.

2 Place the cake in the centre of the cake board and drizzle with a little rum or brandy. Follow steps 3 – 5 for "Covering a Flat Round Cake" to marzipan it.

3 Smooth the marzipan into place and trim away any excess from around the base. Brush both the cake and exposed cake board with the cooled boiled water.

4 Dust your work surface with icing sugar and knead the sugarpaste until pliable. Roll it out and place over the top of the marzipan and board.

5 Smooth the icing in place, smoothing it over the top, sides and board. Trim and neaten around the edges of the board.

Covering the board around the base of a round cake

In some of the designs, such as "Harassed Mum" and "Teddies" I have covered the exposed board around the base of the cake. If you are pushed for time or you feel it looks too fiddly to do then leave it plain. "Stars" and "Tree" both look fine standing on a plain undecorated board.

Place some ribbon around the side of the cake to finish it off or lay a twisted sugarpaste strip around the board as I've done on "Angels".

1 To cover the board, lightly brush a little water over the exposed cake board.

2 Dust your work surface with icing sugar and knead about 200g (7oz) white sugarpaste until it's soft. Roll it into a sausage about 25cm (10in) long.

3 Flatten the sausage with a rolling pin so that it lengthens and becomes a long thin strip about 64cm (25in) long. Be liberal with the icing sugar on your work surface. You do not want the strip to stick to it.

4 Cut a little off one long side of the strip to neaten it. This will form the edge that will butt up against the side of the cake.

5 Slide a knife under one end of the strip and run it under the icing to make sure it's not stuck to your work surface.

6 Roll the icing up like a loose bandage.

7 Starting from the back, unwind the "bandage" around the board. Trim and neaten the join and edges.

Marzipan and Sugarpaste Recipes

Marzipan Recipe

To save time and also because they are so good nowadays, I use ready-made marzipan (almond paste) from the supermarket. I also prefer to use shop bought marzipan because I am cautious about using raw eggs due to the possible risk of salmonella. Here is a recipe if you prefer to make your own. It was given to me by fellow cake decorator Valerie Hedgethorne. In it, the eggs are lightly cooked.

Ingredients

1 whole egg plus 1 extra egg yolk
110g (4oz / ½ cup) caster sugar (superfine sugar)
110g (4oz / 3 cups) icing sugar (confectioners' sugar)
225g (8oz / 2 cups) ground almonds
A few drops of almond essence

Method

1 Put both sugars and the eggs into a heatproof bowl and place over a pan of hot water. Whisk until thick and creamy.

2 Remove the bowl from the heat and add a few drops of almond essence.

3 Stir in the ground almonds then lightly knead into a ball. The marzipan will firm up as it cools but if you feel it is still too soft, add a little more icing sugar

Use as soon as possible. If you need to store it, double wrap it in two small plastic bags or cling film and store in the refrigerator. Use within a week.

Marzipan can be coloured using food colour and used to make models in just the same way as sugarpaste can.

Sugarpaste Recipe

I have only used sugarpaste (rolled fondant) to both cover and decorate the cakes in this book. This is because it is an extremely easy type of icing to use even for the complete beginner. Sugarpaste is available from supermarkets, cake decorating shops (look up your nearest in the phone book) or via mail order. I always use shop-bought sugarpaste but it is perfectly possible to make your own if you prefer.

Ingredients

500g (1lb 2oz / 5 cups) icing sugar (confectioners' sugar)

1 egg white* (or equivalent amount of dried egg white (meringue powder) reconstituted)

30ml (2 tbsp) liquid glucose (available from cake decorating equipment shops, some supermarkets and chemist/ drug stores)

*The consumption of raw egg carries a risk of salmonella particularly for pregnant women, children and the elderly. This risk does not apply to dried egg white.

Method

1 Put the sugar in a large bowl and make a well in the centre.

2 Tip the egg white (or reconstituted egg white / meringue powder) and glucose into the centre and stir in using a knife.

3 Use your hand to finish binding the icing together and knead until the icing feels silky smooth.

4 Double wrap the icing in two small plastic food bags to stop it drying out. It can be used straight away and does not need to be kept in a refrigerator. Use it up within a week.

Cakes covered with sugarpaste should be stored in tins or cardboard cake boxes.

Do not put in airtight plastic containers or they will sweat.

Do not store cakes covered with sugarpaste in the fridge.

Modelling and Colouring Sugarpaste

Modelling

As well as covering cakes, sugarpaste is excellent for making models. To use it successfully, there are a few basic rules you need to follow.

1 Once its packet is opened, it will dry out when not in use so keep any unused icing tightly wrapped in small polythene food bags in a plastic container. It does not need to be kept in a fridge.

2 Always keep a bowl of icing sugar handy when using it. This is both for rolling the sugarpaste out on prior to covering a cake and also for stopping your fingers from becoming sticky.

3 Don't worry about getting dusty icing sugar marks on your models. Once you have finished your design, you simply brush them away with a soft damp paintbrush. The sugarpaste will look shiny for a while but it will eventually revert back to a matt finish.

4 For sticking your models together you can just use little light dabs of cooled boiled water.

Colouring Sugarpaste

You can buy ready-coloured sugarpaste from cake decorating shops, some supermarkets and via mail order but it is easy to colour your own.

Try to use paste or gel colours (available from the same outlets as above) as these are thicker than liquid colourings and won't make your icing soggy.

Simply apply some dabs of food colour paste to the sugarpaste. For hygiene reasons, use a new cocktail stick (toothpick) to do this and throw it away afterwards.

If you want to achieve a marbled effect, stop kneading while veins of colour are clearly visible. Otherwise continue kneading until the icing has turned a flat matt colour with no streaks.

You can also mix different colours of sugarpaste together such as a lump of red and yellow to make orange or white and black to make grey. To lighten a colour, knead in more white.

Flesh Tones

To make a pink flesh colour, either use a shade of food paste called "paprika" or knead a little pink, yellow and white sugarpaste together.

For darker tones, use a brown food colour paste or knead a little green, red and black sugarpaste together. For the teddy bears on page 22, use a shade of food colour paste called "Autumn Leaf". It is also possible to buy a ready coloured sugarpaste called Teddy Bear Brown. Alternatively knead some red, yellow and a little black sugarpaste together or knead yellow, red and black food colour paste into a blob of white sugarpaste.

Christmas Roses

This is the simplest method I can find to make roses but it is not the only one. If you prefer to use a different method then feel free to do so. If you're feeling really extravagant you could even use real blooms!

You will need

1 X 20cm (8in) round iced cake on a 25cm (10in) round iced cake board (See page 8 and 9 for quantities and instructions for covering the cake and board)

450g (15oz) red sugarpaste
450g (15oz) green sugarpaste
1 heaped teaspoon icing sugar

Icing sugar for rolling out on
Water for sticking

Equipment

Rolling pin
Small sharp knife
Paintbrush
Template for leaf
1m ribbon
Scissors
Sieve or tea strainer

fig 1

TIP: If you have a large rose leaf cutter, you could use that instead to speed up the leaf making process.

To decorate your cake

1 Take about 30g (1oz) red sugarpaste and roll it into a sausage shape. Dust your work surface with icing sugar and flatten the sausage with a rolling pin.

2 Cut away a little sugarpaste from one long side to leave a neat, straight edge behind. (fig 1). Scrunch up and re-use this leftover red icing.

3 Slide your knife along under the strip to make sure it's not stuck to your work surface and paint a light line of water along the uneven edge of the strip.

4 Slowly roll the rose up like a loose bandage.

5 Pinch the base together. This should force the top to open slightly. Open up the rose still more with your fingers. Pinch and tweak the rose into shape.

6 Cut a little sugarpaste off the bottom to make a nice flat base for your rose to sit on. Place and stick it on top of your cake. Re-use the leftover red.

7 Make about another 15 roses and place in a ring around the outer edge of the cake.

8 To make a leaf, thinly roll out about 30g (1oz) green sugarpaste.

9 Cut out a simple leaf shape using the template if necessary. (fig 2).

10 Press a few veins into the leaf using the back of your knife.

11 Lay and stick the leaf between or around one of the roses.

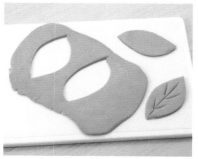

fig 2

12 Repeat making about another 30 leaves.

13 Place a heaped teaspoon of icing sugar in a tea strainer or sieve and gently tap and shape the sugar over the top of the cake.

14 Place some ribbon around the base of the cake and secure at the back with a little sticky tape. Make a bow and stick in place with a blob of sticky sugarpaste.

TIP: You could easily adapt this design to make an attractive birthday cake by simply changing the colour of the roses to yellow or pink.

TIP: Add more thinner ribbon around the edge of the board if you wish. Hold in place with double sided tape.

Santa and Rudolph

To simplify this design, lose Rudolph and just have Santa. You could even lose most of Santa himself – make a bigger mound of icing snowballs than the one shown and poke a head and arm out. (See page 1)

You will need

1 irregular shaped 20cm (8in) iced cake on a 25cm (10in) round cake board (see page 9 for quantities and instructions for covering the cake and board)

90g (3oz) red coloured sugarpaste
250g (8oz) white sugarpaste
30g (1oz) flesh coloured sugarpaste
10g (⅓ oz) black sugarpaste
60g (2 oz) brown coloured sugarpaste
Black food colour or black food colour pen
1 strand raw, uncooked spaghetti
Icing sugar for rolling out on
Water for sticking

Equipment

Paintbrush
Small rolling pin (or you can use your paintbrush as one)
Small sharp non-serrated knife

fig 1

TIP: Use the snowballs to hide any problem areas on the cake You could also make a few penguins or fairies.

To decorate your cake

1 Roll 60g (2oz) red sugarpaste into a cone shape for Santa's body (fig 1) Stick on cake. Insert short length of spaghetti for support.

2 Make a 15g (½ oz) flesh coloured sugarpaste oval head. Stick on body. Roll 10g (⅓ oz) black sugarpaste into a sausage about 6cm (2in) long for his boots. Cut in half and bend each into an "L" shape. Stick in place and press a few lines in each sole with the back of knife.

3 Make a 30g (1oz) white sugarpaste sausage about 16cm (6in) long and lay and stick around base of Santa. Use end of paintbrush to poke a few hollows into the trim. Make a 5g (⅛ oz) red sugarpaste triangle for his hat and stick on head.

4 For his beard, thinly roll out about 5g (⅛ oz) white sugarpaste. Press lines into it and cut out a triangle. Stick on front of his face. Poke a hole with the end of a paintbrush for mouth. Make two diamond shapes for moustache and stick on top of mouth. Tweak ends slightly.

5 Make three tiny flesh coloured balls for nose and ears. Stick in place and poke end of a paintbrush in each ear. Lay a thin white sausage around hat base. Add pom-pom and hollows as before.

6 Make 15g (½ oz) brown sugarpaste cone for his sack. Pinch around narrowest end to open it up. Stick against Santa's body. Poke line of stitching down centre of sack with knife tip.

7 Make a 10g (⅓ oz) red sausage for arms and cut in half. Stick in place against the body and sack. Make two white discs for cuffs and two flesh ones for hands. Stick on arms.

8 Roll 45g (1½ oz) white sugarpaste into about 8 balls. Stick in a pile next to Santa.

9 Roll about 30g (1oz) brown sugarpaste into a sausage about 5cm (2in) long for Rudolph (fig 2). Pinch two ears into one end. Make a tiny brown sausage for arm and stick poking out of snowdrift.

10 Make a tiny flesh coloured sausage for horns. Stick on head between ears. Use end of paintbrush to lightly press the icing in place. The two ends should automatically bend up to make horns.

fig 2

11 Make four tiny white balls for eyes. Stick two on each character's face. Paint black food colour dot on each one. Stick red sugarpaste ball on Rudolph for his trademark red nose. Make leftover white sugarpaste into snowballs and stick around cake.

TIP: Place a spoonful of icing sugar in a tea strainer or sieve and gently sprinkle over the finished cake to look like snow.

Snowmen

This particular cake I sat on a 30cm (12in) round cake board. The only reason for this was so that it gave me more space around the base of the cake to stand the snowmen. The design will work just as well on a smaller 25cm (10in) board. Just make the snowmen round the sides a little less portly!

You will need

1 irregular-shaped iced 20cm (8in) cake on a 30cm (12in) or 25cm (10in) round cake board.
(See page 9 for quantities and instructions for covering the cake and board).

500g (1lb 2oz) white sugarpaste
210g (7oz) green sugarpaste
45g (1½ oz) red sugarpaste
10g (⅓ oz) orange coloured sugarpaste
2-3 strands raw, uncooked spaghetti broken into 7cm (3in) lengths
Black food colour paste
Icing sugar for rolling out on
Water for sticking

Equipment

Rolling pin
Small sharp knife
Paintbrush

TIP: Position the snowballs to hide any imperfections or marks on your cake.

To decorate your cake

1   To make a snowman, first roll 30g (1oz) white sugarpaste into an oval for his body. Stand him on the cake and insert a short length of uncooked spaghetti to provide additional support. (fig 1) Leave about 2.5cm (1in) protruding.

fig 1

2   Roll about 10g (⅓ oz) white sugarpaste into a ball for his head and stick on top of the body.

3   Thinly roll out about 30g (1oz) of green sugarpaste for his scarf. (fig 2) Cut out two rectangles about 4cm X 1.5cm (1½ in X ½ in). Press lines across both rectangles with the back of a knife. Cut a fringe into one end.

4   Stick one rectangle around the snowman's neck then stick the other section on top with the fringe hanging down.

5   Shape about 5g (⅛ oz) red sugarpaste into a triangle for his hat. Bend the tip to one side slightly and stick on his head.

6   Make a tiny orange carrot shape for his nose and stick onto his face.

7   Roll about 5g (⅛ oz) white sugarpaste into a sausage for the hat's trim and stick around hat base. Add a tiny white sugarpaste ball for the hat's pop-pom.

8   Make two small white sausage shapes for arms and stick them in whatever position you like.

Repeat the procedure making another six snowmen.

fig 2

9   Using a fine paintbrush and a little black food paste, paint dots for the snowmen's eyes, mouth and buttons.

10   Roll the leftover white sugarpaste into different sized snowballs and stick around the top and sides of the cake.

TIP: You can use a food colour pen to make the eyes, mouth and buttons if you prefer. But allow the snowmen to harden if using one so that the pen's point doesn't poke into the sugarpaste and damage the snowman's complexion!

Angels

To make the Angels stand out, I kneaded a little blue food colour into the sugarpaste before covering the cake, however you can leave it white if you prefer. The decoration around the base of the cake is simply a strip of twisted suparpaste. This is a quick and easy way to finish off a cake if you do not want to pipe or use ribbon.

You will need

1 pale blue coloured iced cake on a 25cm (10in) round cake board
(see page 8 for quantities and instructions for covering the cake itself)

350g (12oz) white sugarpaste
90g (3oz) flesh coloured sugarpaste
30g (1oz) brown sugarpaste
30g (1oz) yellow sugarpaste
2 strands raw, uncooked spaghetti
Black food colour or black food colour pen
3 sheets rice paper (edible wafer paper)
Icing sugar for rolling out on
Water for sticking

Equipment

Small sharp knife
Fine paintbrush
Pencil
Scissors
Rolling pin
Wing template

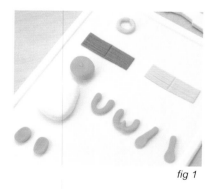

fig 1

TIP: Use a small strip of moist sugarpaste to hold the wings in place if they keep falling off.

To decorate your cake

1 Roll 45g (1 ½ oz) white sugarpaste into a conical shape for an Angel's dress (fig 1) and stand on cake.

2 Poke a short length of spaghetti through body into cake for support. Roll 10g (⅓ oz) flesh coloured sugarpaste into a ball and stick on top of body.

3 For arms, roll 10g (⅓ oz) flesh coloured sugarpaste into a sausage about 5cm (2in) long and stick in a "U" shape on front of Angel.

4 For hair, thinly roll out about 15g (½ oz) yellow or brown sugarpaste. Cut out a rectangle about 8cm X 2cm (3in X ⅔ in). Press lines into it using back of knife. Lay and stick on head.

5 Press a centre parting in top of Angel's hair with the back of a knife. Make a thin yellow sugarpaste string for the halo. Bend it into a ring shape. Stick on head.

6 Paint two dots for eyes and stick a tiny flesh coloured ball below them for a nose. Paint a "U" shape for a mouth.

7 For wings, fold a piece of rice paper in half and with fold on the dotted line, trace over the wing template. (fig 2) Cut out. Open up the wings and gently press into the back of the Angel.

8 Make another two Angels. For arms in a praying position, fold a 10g (⅓ oz) flesh coloured sugarpaste sausage shape in half and pinch the centre together. Pull the two ends apart so that the icing forms a "W" shape.

9 For the sitting down Angel, make a white conical shape as before but this time, bend her in half and sit on the cake.

10 Make two small flesh coloured oval shapes for her feet and stick on base of her dress. Make two small thin sausage shapes for her arms and stick one either side of the body. Add head, hair, halo, wings and features as before.

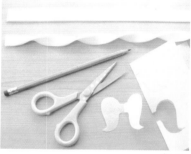

fig 2

11 Paint a light line of water around the exposed cake board around the base of the cake and roll 200g (7oz) white sugarpaste into a long white sausage.

12 Flatten sausage and cut out a strip about 60cm X 1.5cm (24in X ½ in). Slide a knife under the strip to stop it sticking. Carefully twist the sugarpaste. Lift and lay it round board.

13 Cut out some rice paper clouds and stick around cake with a little water.

TIP: If you don't feel confident about painting a smile, hold a drinking straw at a slight angle and press it into the Angel's face to leave a "U" shaped impression.

Harassed Mum !

This one came from the heart ! I have dressed the mum in Jeans so that you could easily adapt the figure to make a harassed dad instead. Change the hair colour and other features to make it more personal to your own harassed relative !

You will need

1 X 20cm (8in) round iced cake on a 25cm (10in) round iced cake board (see page 8 & 9 for quantities and instructions for covering the cake and board.)

75g (2½ oz) red sugarpaste
60g (2oz) blue sugarpaste
100g (3½ oz) white sugarpaste
30g (1oz) flesh coloured sugarpaste
75g (2½) brown sugarpaste
60g (2oz) green sugarpaste
1 strand raw, uncooked spaghetti
Icing sugar for rolling out on
Water for sticking

Equipment

Rolling pin
Small sharp knife
Fine paintbrush
1m ribbon
Scissors
Sticky tape

fig 1

TIP: You could also make a toy penguin too if you wish. Follow the instructions for making a penguin on page 32.

To decorate your cake

1 Thinly roll out about 60g (2oz) red sugarpaste for the rug and cut out a rectangle about 15cm X 8cm (6in X 3in). Press lines across it with the back of your knife and fringe the ends. Stick on cake.

2 Roll 60g (2oz) blue sugarpaste into a sausage about 20cm (8in) long for her legs. Bend into a "U" shape (fig 1) and stick on rug.

3 For her body, make a 45g (1½ oz) white sugarpaste oval and stick on trousers. For added support, insert a short length of spaghetti. Leave a little protruding.

4 Make a 5g (⅛ oz) white oval for the jumper's neck. Press a few vertical lines around its edge and stick in place. Add a 15g (½ oz) flesh coloured ball for her head.

5 Thinly roll out 15g (½ oz) brown sugarpaste for her hair. Cut out a small rectangle and press lines down its length. Stick over head.

6 Make two brown 5g (⅛ oz) oval shapes for shoes and stick on end of legs. Press the back of a knife into the sole of each shoe a few times.

7 Roll about 20g (⅔ oz) brown sugarpaste into an oval for the turkey (fig 2). Add two flattish oval shapes for legs. Put the turkey on the cake and stick two tiny white ovals on each leg in a "T" shape.

8 Make two 10g (⅓ oz) white sausage shapes for mum's arms. Stick them in place. Add two small flesh coloured discs for hands.

fig 2

9 Stick a tiny ball of flesh coloured sugarpaste on her face for a nose and paint three black food colour dots and two lines for her eyes and mouth.

10 For her hat, make a 5g (⅛ oz) red triangle. Stick on head. Roll 5g (⅛ oz) white sugarpaste into a sausage and stick around hat. Add tiny white pom-pom.

11 Make squares and rectangles for presents and press a cross into each one with the back of a knife. Make at least six in different colours.

12 For wrapping paper, roll about 20g (⅔ oz) sugarpaste out flat and cut out a rectangle about 5cm X 8cm (2 X 3 in). Carefully roll the "paper" up and stick on to the cake. Make about three in different colours.

13 To make a teddy bear, follow the instructions for a teddy on page 22 but reduce the size. Place ribbon round base of cake to finish and secure at back with sticky tape.

Teddies

You could simplify this design and just have one teddy one if you want. You can also make your teddies any colour you like. Change the message and this would also make a cute birthday or Christening design. If you cannot get hold of sandwich flags, make your own by sticking a small paper rectangle to a cocktail stick or drinking straw.

You will need

1 X 20cm (8in) round iced cake on a 25cm (10in) round iced cake board (see pages 8 and 9 for quantities and instructions for covering the cake and board)

300g (10oz) golden brown coloured sugarpaste (see page 11 for colouring tips)
45g (1 ½ oz) white sugarpaste
10g (⅓ oz) red sugarpaste
2 X 7cm (3in) lengths uncooked spaghetti (break a long one to size)
Black food colour paste
Icing sugar for rolling out on
Water for sticking

Equipment

Small paintbrush
Small rolling pin (optional)
Small, sharp, non-serrated knife
2 sandwich flags
Pen for writing message
1m ribbon for decoration

fig 1

TIP: For simpler features, paint black dots for the eyes and nose and press the edge of a drinking straw held at an angle into the muzzle to give your bear a smile.

To decorate your cake

1 Roll 60g (2oz) brown sugarpaste into a cone shape (fig 1). Flatten the top slightly and stick onto the cake with a small dab of water.

2 Roll a pea-sized lump of white sugarpaste into a ball. Flatten it into a thin disc with small rolling pin or paintbrush used as one and stick onto the teddy's tummy. For extra support, stick a bit of spaghetti into the teddy's body leaving about 2.5cm (1in) protruding.

3 Roll about 20g (¾ oz) brown sugarpaste into a ball for his head. Stick onto body. Roll 15g (½ oz) brown sugarpaste into a sausage about 8cm (3in) long for his legs. Cut it in half and bend each one into an "L" shape and stick in place.

4 Press four hollows into sole of each foot with end of paintbrush. Roll 15g (½ oz) brown sugarpaste into a sausage for his arms. Cut in half and stick in place.

5 Make a small white oval for his muzzle and two white sugarpaste balls for his eyes and stick in place. Make two tiny brown balls for his ears and stick on head. Poke a hollow in each ear with the end of a paintbrush.

6 Make a 5g (⅛ oz) red triangle for his hat and stick on his head. Roll about 10g (⅓ oz) white sugarpaste into a thin string and stick around base of hat. Add tiny white pom-pom.

7 Paint eyes, nose and mouth on the teddy's face with black food colour.

fig 2

8 For second teddy, make body as before (fig 2) but lay it on the edge of the cake. Make two 10g (⅓ oz) sausage shapes for arms and stick on the cake. Stick a 20g (⅔ oz) brown ball for his head on top of the arms and body.

9 Make another two legs. Bend one into an "S" shape and stick it on the side of the teddy's body. Shape the other into an "L" shape and stick so it hangs down the side of the cake.

10 Make ears, muzzle and a hat as before and paint a nose and mouth on the face.

11 Write your message on the flags and gently place into position. Finish your cake off with a bit of ribbon.

TIP: To get the stripey effect I used two different widths of ribbon placed on top of each other and secured at the back with a little sticky tape.

Nativity

Sitting icing characters on the edge of a cake is a nice way of giving them a bit of height but without the trauma of trying to make them stand up. You could substitute other figures in place of those shown if you wanted. Santa and Rudolph with presents instead of sheep for example.

You will need

1 X 20cm (8in) round iced cake on a 25cm (10in) round iced cake board (see page 8 and 9 for quantities and instructions for covering the cake and board.)

75g (2 ½ oz) brown coloured sugarpaste
45g (1½ oz) pale blue coloured sugarpaste
45g (1 ½ oz) flesh-coloured sugarpaste
125g (4oz) white sugarpaste
1 strand raw, uncooked spaghetti
Black food colour or food colour pen
30g (1oz) Demerara sugar

Equipment

Paintbrush
Rolling pin
Small sharp knife
Spoon

fig 1

TIP: If you don't want to use sugar, dab watered down food colour around the cake instead.

To decorate your cake

1 Make a 45g (1 ½ oz) brown sugarpaste cone for Joseph's body (fig 1). Flatten it slightly and bend into an "S" shape. Sit on front edge of cake. Stick a bit of spaghetti vertically through the body for support. Repeat the same procedure with 45g pale blue sugarpaste for Mary (fig 2).

2 Make a 10g (⅓ oz) white sugarpaste oval for baby Jesus. Squash a small ball of flesh coloured sugarpaste and stick on one end. Add a tiny flesh coloured dot for a nose and paint two tiny "U" shapes for eyes.

3 Make a 5g (⅛ oz) brown sausage shape for Joseph's arm and a slightly thinner flesh coloured sausage for Mary's arm. Place baby between them and stick their arms in position. Make a small flesh coloured oval hand and stick on end of Joseph's arm.

4 Make a 10g (⅓ oz) flesh coloured ball for Joseph's head. Stick in place. Thinly roll out about 15g (½ oz) brown sugarpaste and press lines into it using the back of your knife. Cut out a small triangle for his beard and two tiny leaf shapes for his moustache and stick on his face.

5 Add a small flesh coloured ball for his nose. For his headdress, thinly roll out about 10g (⅓ oz) brown sugarpaste and cut out a rectangle about 8cm X 3cm (3in X 1in) Drape and stick over head.

6 Make a ball for Mary's head and stick it in place. For her hair, cut out a flat brown rectangle. Press a few lines into it. Lay over her head and press a central parting in it using the back of your knife. Make a white headdress and drape over her head.

fig 2

7 Make a tiny ball for Mary's nose. Paint two black dots on each face for eyes and give both characters two small flesh coloured oval shaped feet.

8 For a sheep, make a 10g (⅓ oz) white oval. Poke a few hollows into it with end of a paintbrush. Squash a small ball of black sugarpaste into an oval. Pinch two ears into top and stick on body. Add two tiny white sugarpaste balls for eyes. Paint black dot on each eye.

9 Make as many sheep as you want. (Use them to hide any marks or blemishes on the cake surface) and stick around the top and side of the cake.

10 To finish, lightly dab a little water around the base of the cake and spoon a little Demerera sugar around the base and top of the cake.

TIP: If you're feeling particularly adventurous, you could make some cows and pigs too.

Christmas Pudding Village

To make life easier I have used a bit of specialist equipment on this one – a small holly cutter. These are readily available in kitchen or cake decorating equipment shops towards the end of the year. Cutters are also available by mail order via the internet. However don't despair if you still can't get hold of one. A method for making your own holly leaves is shown on the Fairy cake on page 30. Just make smaller versions of the ones shown on that design.

You will need

1 irregular shaped iced 20cm (8in) cake
on a 25cm (10in) round cake board
(See page 9 for quantities and
instructions for covering the cake itself)

300g (10oz) dark brown sugarpaste
30g (1oz) light brown sugarpaste*
45g (1½ oz) cream coloured sugarpaste*
15g (½ oz) black sugarpaste
150g (5oz) white sugarpaste
45g (1½ oz) green sugarpaste
30g (1oz) red sugarpaste
Black food colour paste
1 sheet rice paper (edible wafer paper)
Icing sugar for rolling out on
Water for sticking

*See "Tip" below

Equipment

Rolling pin
Small sharp knife
Fine paintbrush
Door and cream topping templates
if required
Small holly cutter (optional –
see introduction above)
Scissors

TIP: To make cream coloured sugarpaste, knead a little yellow into some white. Likewise, to make light brown coloured sugarpaste, knead some white sugarpaste into a bit of the dark brown.

TIP: Use the snowballs strategically to hide any marks or imperfections.

To decorate your cake

1 To make a pudding, roll 100g (3½ oz) brown sugarpaste into a ball. (fig 1)

2 Thinly roll out about 5g (⅛ oz) light brown sugarpaste. Cut out a door shape. Press vertical lines into the door using the back of a knife. Stick the door onto the front of the pudding.

3 Paint simple arched window shapes either side of the door with black food colour. Paint a cross in the middle of each window.

4 Thinly roll out about 15g (½ oz) cream coloured sugarpaste. Cut out a wavy-edged circular shape. Use template if necessary. Stick on top of the pudding. Make a tiny cream coloured ball for the door knocker and stick on the door.

5 Make some tiny black ball shapes for the currants and press and stick around the pudding.

6 Stick a tiny strip of white icing "snow" over the top of the door.

7 Place the house in position on the cake and make two steps by sticking two thin strips of light brown icing on top of each other in front of the door.

8 Thinly roll out about 10g (⅓ oz) green sugarpaste. Cut out three holly leaves and press veins into them with the back of a knife. Stick the holly leaves on top of the house. Add three tiny red icing balls for the berries. Make another two houses.

9 Make three little fairies (fig 2) See the Fairy design on page 30 for instructions.

fig 1

10 Make some white sugarpaste "snowballs" and stick around the base and between the houses.

fig 2

Tip: You could sieve some icing sugar "snow" over your village if you wish.

TIP: For a sparkly door knocker, use an edible gold or silver ball.

Christmas Stars

If you can wield a pair of scissors you should be alright with this one! You could make the stars stand out even more by colouring the sugarpaste covering the cake a pale blue colour as on the "Angels" design. If you're bothered by the amount of exposed cake board on view, you can cover that as well. Instructions for how to do this are given on page 9.

You will need

1 X 20cm (8in) round iced cake on a 25cm (10in) round cake board
(See page 8 for quantities and instructions for covering the cake.)

30g (1oz) white sugarpaste
8/9 sheets rice paper (edible wafer paper)
Edible silver ball cake decorations
Water

Equipment

Small sharp knife
2/3 sheets paper kitchen towel
80cm (31in) ribbon
Sticky tape (optional)
Scissors
Ruler
Pencil
Star templates (page 36)

fig 1

TIP: When cutting out the stars, try to cut just inside the pencil marks so they won't show.

To decorate your cake

1 Using a clean damp cloth or piece of kitchen paper, carefully clean the exposed cake board around the iced cake, trying not to dent the sides of the cake with an over enthusiastic knuckle! Dry it using a second piece of paper towel.

2 Place the ribbon around the base of the cake. Secure it at the back using a small blob of damp, sticky sugarpaste or a little sticky tape.

3 Place a sheet of rice paper over the large star template and trace over it using a ruler and pencil. Repeat and cut out eight large stars. (fig 1) Make eleven middle-sized stars and three small stars.

4 To assemble a star, place a tiny damp, tacky ball of sugarpaste in the centre of a large star and place a middle-sized star on top. Just roll a little sugarpaste in your fingers with a drop of water. Don't soak it or your star will dissolve. Just dampen it enough to make it sticky and gluey. (fig 2).

5 Place another tiny, damp sugarpaste ball on top and press an edible silver ball into it. Make another seven large / middle sized star combinations.

6 Make two middle size/small star combinations and one small / small combination.

7 Gently arrange one large/middle-sized star, two middle-sized/small stars and the one small/small star on top of the cake. Stand the remaining stars around the outside of the cake.

fig 2

8 Carefully stick the stars in place using more small damp balls of sticky sugarpaste.

9 Press a few extra silver balls into the cake between the stars. If they won't stick, glue them in place using more small damp balls of sugarpaste.

TIP: Arrange the stars so that they hide any imperfections in the cake's surface.

TIP: You could alter this design to suit other occasions.

Colour the sugarpaste pink and cut out rice paper hearts for Valentines Day, for example.

Fairies

The holly leaves on this cake have all been individually made. They look stylish and bold and are actually very simple to do. However if you want to make life really easy for yourself, you could buy a ready-shaped holly cutter from a high street or mail order cake decorating equipment shop.

You will need

1 X 20cm (8in) round iced cake on a 25cm (10in) round iced cake board (see pages 8 & 9 for quantities and instructions for covering the cake and board.)

500g (1lb 2oz) green coloured sugarpaste
100g (3 ½ oz) flesh coloured sugarpaste
60g (2oz) yellow sugarpaste
100g (3 ½ oz) red sugarpaste
60g (2oz) white sugarpaste
Black food colour paste or pen
2 sheets rice paper (edible wafer paper)
Icing sugar for rolling out
Water for sticking

Equipment

Rolling pin
Small sharp knife
Small round lid or cutter
Paintbrush
Scissors

fig 1

TIP: When cutting out a holly leaf, hold your knife almost vertical. You are less likely to tear the sugarpaste that way.

To decorate your cake

1 To make a holly leaf, thinly roll out about 20g (⅔ oz) green sugarpaste. Cut out a simple leaf shape (fig 1)

2 Using a small lid or round cutter take "bites" out of both sides of the leaf.

3 Press a few veins into the leaf using the back of your knife and stick onto the cake with a light dab of water. You will need 22-25 leaves in total to stick around the top and base of the cake.

4 To make a fairy, first roll about 5g (⅛ oz) flesh coloured sugarpaste into a thin string for her legs. (fig 2) Bend it in half and stick them on the cake.

5 Make a small 5g (⅛ oz) green icing triangle shape for her body and stick on top of her legs.

6 Make a 5g (⅛ oz) flesh coloured ball for her head and stick on top of the body. Make two tiny arms and stick them in place. (Holding a holly leaf is nice)

7 For her hair, thinly roll out about 10g (⅓ oz) yellow sugarpaste. Cut out a small rectangle and lay and stick over her head. Scrunch up and re-use the leftover yellow.

8 Make a small red triangle for her hat. Stick on top of her head. Stick a thin string of white sugarpaste around the hat's base and a bobble on the end.

9 Fold a bit of rice paper in half. With the fold in the middle, cut out half a heart shape. Open it up to make a heart shaped pair of wings. Gently press the fold of the wings into the back of the fairy.

10 Add two black food colour dots for eyes. Make another 8-10 fairies.

11 For the berries, roll the leftover red coloured sugarpaste into balls and stick around the leaves and fairies.

fig 2

TIP: Make the leaves as you need them.

This makes them easier to drape around the fairies. If you make all 25 in one go, you may find they start drying out and crack as you position them.

TIP: If you have time you could make and place other Christmas models, such as small presents or Christmas puddings amongst the leaves.

Penguins

At first glance you may think this quite a complicated design but that's just because of the number of things on the cake. Pull a penguin apart and you will see that it is actually made up of easy to make shapes – a sausage and a few balls and triangles.

You will need

1 irregular – shaped iced cake on a 25cm (10in) round cake board (see page 9 for quantities and instructions for covering the cake and board.)

120g (4oz) black sugarpaste
30g (1oz) orange coloured sugarpaste
45g (1½ oz) red sugarpaste
150g (5oz) white sugarpaste
30g (1oz) green sugarpaste
Black food colour paste
Blue food colour paste (optional)
Icing sugar for rolling out on
Water for sticking

Equipment

Rolling pin
Small sharp knife
Paintbrush

fig 1

TIP: If you find it easier, use a black food colour pen to make the dots on the eyes.

TIP: Use snowballs to hide any damaged or unsightly bits on the cake itself !

To decorate your cake

1 To make a basic penguin, roll 15g (½ oz) black sugarpaste into a thick sausage shape. (fig 1) (You can vary the amounts of black sugarpaste for each penguin to make different sized ones.) You will need about 7-8 penguins in all.

2 Make two small orange sugarpaste carrot shapes for his feet and squash them into flattish triangles. Stand and stick the penguin's body on the feet.

3 Make two tiny white sugarpaste balls for his eyes and a larger pea-sized one for his tummy. Squash the tummy one flat. Stick the tummy and eyes in place. Paint two black food colour dots on his eyes.

4 Make a tiny orange triangle for his beak and two small black ones for wings. Stick in place. Make a red triangle for his hat and stick on head. Roll a little white sugarpaste into a thin string and stick around base of hat. Add white pom-pom.

5 For the pond, take 30g (1oz) white sugarpaste and 5g (⅛ oz) black (or a tiny bit of black food colour paste). Knead together until a marbled effect begins to appear. Break off little bits and roll into small misshapen rock shapes. Paint a line of water on top of cake in shape of pond and stick the "rocks" in place.

6 For penguins in pond, make one whole one and cut in half. Place both halves flat side down in the pond. Take about 5g (⅛ oz) white sugarpaste and roll it into a sausage. Wet it and squidge it between your fingers until it's very sticky and lay it around the base of one of the penguins.

7 Using the wrong end of your paintbrush, carefully stroke and draw the soggy

sugarpaste up the penguin's body so that it looks like splashy water. (fig 2) Repeat on the other penguin and dab a little watered down blue food colour on the water's surface if you wish.

fig 2

8 To make a towel, thinly roll out about 15g (½ oz) green sugarpaste. Cut out a rectangle. Press lines into the rectangle using the back of your knife and cut a fringe into the two thin ends. Either stick in place on the cake and place a penguin on top sunbathing or roll it up and place under a penguin's wing.

9 Roll any leftover white sugarpaste into snowballs and stick around the top and sides of the cake.

Christmas Tree

**Although it looks very simple, this design took me ages to put together.
The reason for this was that it was originally quite an ornate and fussy cake but it just didn't look right.
I kept taking things off it and found that as is often the case – less is much much more.**

You will need

1 X 20 cm (8in) round iced cake on a 25cm (10in) round cake board (see page 8 for quantities and instructions for covering the cake.)

200g (7oz) white sugarpaste
1 pack edible gold or silver balls
Icing sugar for rolling out on
Water for sticking

Equipment

Rolling pin
Tree & tub templates if required
Paintbrush
Cocktail stick
70cm (28in) ribbon for side of cake
Sticky tape

fig 1

Tip: If you can't find gold balls, silver ones will work just as well. You can even get coloured ones from specialist cake decorating shops.

To decorate your cake

1 Trace and cut out the tree template (fig 1).

2 Dust your work surface with icing sugar and knead and roll out the white sugarpaste to a thickness of about 4mm (¼ in).

3 Place the tree template on top and carefully cut around it. (fig 2)

4 Stick the tree in place on top of the cake with a little water.

5 Cut out the tub shape and stick on the cake beneath the tree. Leave about a 5mm (¼ in) gap between the top of the tub and the base of the tree.

6 Lightly paint over the tree with a little water. Be careful. Try not to drip onto the cake surface or you'll get hollow water marks.

7 Using the wrong end of your paintbrush, scratch and pull lines into the tree. Start at the top and work down. Try not to lean on the cake itself (fig 3)

8 Repeat using the cocktail stick to add some finer marks.

9 Press one gold ball with five around it into the icing at the top of the tree to make the star.

10 Arrange and press the rest of the gold balls into the tree to look like strings of decorations.

11 Stand ribbon around base of cake and secure at the back with a little sticky tape.

fig 2

TIP: If you prefer your baubles less crunchy, you could make sugarpaste balls instead and even make little sugarpaste parcels to decorate your tree.

fig 3

TIP: If you don't like an all white cake you could make the tree out of green sugarpaste instead.

Templates

All templates shown are actual size. Trace and then cut out.

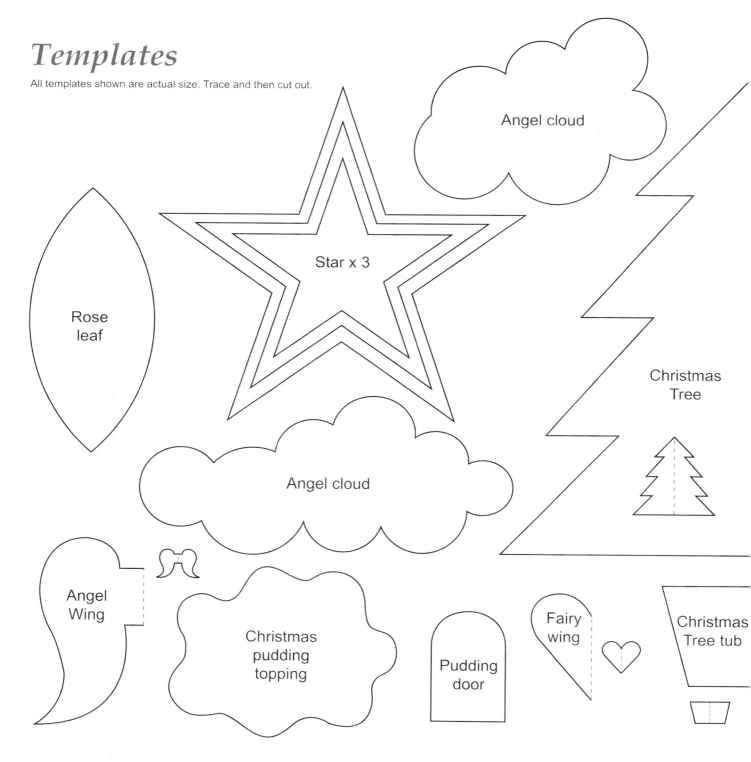

Angel cloud

Rose leaf

Star x 3

Christmas Tree

Angel cloud

Angel Wing

Christmas pudding topping

Pudding door

Fairy wing

Christmas Tree tub